Animal Life Cycles

Activity Book

Name: _____

Age: _____

Class: _____

School: _____

OXFORD
UNIVERSITY PRESS

UNIVERSITY PRESS

Great Clarendon Street, Oxford OX2 6DP

Oxford University Press is a department of the University of Oxford.
It furthers the University's objective of excellence in research, scholarship,
and education by publishing worldwide in

Oxford New York

Auckland Cape Town Dar es Salaam Hong Kong Karachi
Kuala Lumpur Madrid Melbourne Mexico City Nairobi
New Delhi Shanghai Taipei Toronto

With offices in

Argentina Austria Brazil Chile Czech Republic France Greece
Guatemala Hungary Italy Japan Poland Portugal Singapore
South Korea Switzerland Thailand Turkey Ukraine Vietnam

OXFORD and OXFORD ENGLISH are registered trade marks of
Oxford University Press in the UK and in certain other countries

© Oxford University Press 2011

The moral rights of the author have been asserted

Database right Oxford University Press (maker)

First published 2011
2015 2014 2013 2012 2011
10 9 8 7 6 5 4 3 2 1

No unauthorized photocopying

All rights reserved. No part of this publication may be reproduced,
stored in a retrieval system, or transmitted, in any form or by any means,
without the prior permission in writing of Oxford University Press,
or as expressly permitted by law, or under terms agreed with the appropriate
reprographics rights organization. Enquiries concerning reproduction outside
the scope of the above should be sent to the ELT Rights Department, Oxford
University Press, at the address above

You must not circulate this book in any other binding or cover
and you must impose this same condition on any acquirer

Any websites referred to in this publication are in the public domain and
their addresses are provided by Oxford University Press for information only.
Oxford University Press disclaims any responsibility for the content

ISBN: 978 0 19 464512 6

Printed in China

This book is printed on paper from certified and well-managed sources.

ACKNOWLEDGEMENTS

Animal Life Cycles Activity Book by: Alistair McCallum

Illustrations by: Fiammetta Dogi/The Art Agency, Kelly Kennedy, and
Dusan Pavlic/Beehive Illustration

Introduction  Page 3

1 **Circle the correct words.**

1 All /(Some)/ No animals lay eggs.

2 When animals grow up, they can produce **mates / young / tadpoles**.

3 A crocodile carries her babies **in her mouth / on her back / on her feet**.

4 An animal's life cycle starts when it **produces young / lays eggs / is born**.

5 An animal can produce young when it has found **a mate / a baby / an egg**.

6 A tadpole grows into a **bird / kangaroo / frog**.

2 **Answer the questions.**

1 Write the name of one animal that has babies, and one animal that lays eggs.

_____

2 Write the name of one animal that lives in the ocean, and one animal that lives on the land.

_____

3 What is your favorite animal? Why?

_____

_____

1 Life Cycles  Pages 4–7

1 Complete the sentences.

> mollusk   amphibian   arthropod   ~~annelid~~
> reptile   mammal

1 An earthworm is an __annelid__.

2 A frog is an _____.

3 A snail is a _____.

4 A lion is a _____.

5 A spider is an _____.

6 A snake is a _____.

2 Order the words. Then write *true* or *false*.

1 for / very / Life / dangerous / animals. / is

   __Life is very dangerous for animals.__   __true__

2 are / animals that / backbone. / have / Invertebrates / a

   _____   _____

3 the animal / are / species / invertebrates. / the world / in / Most of

   _____   _____

4 than / much / Most vertebrates / smaller / invertebrates. / are

   _____   _____

5 plants and / eat / animals. / Herbivores

   _____   _____

6 for / live / tortoise / 150 / Galapagos / years. / A / can

   _____   _____

3 Match. Then write complete sentences.

people hunt	to baby animals
all animals need to	lay eggs
some animals give birth	birds and other animals
males produce sperm, and	females produce eggs
reptiles and birds	because of pollution
many animals become sick	find food to stay alive

1 People hunt birds and other animals.
2 _____
3 _____
4 _____
5 _____
6 _____

4 Complete the sentences.

1 Vertebrates are animals that have a b a c k b o n e.
2 Animals like crabs that have a hard _ _ _ _ _ are called arthropods.
3 Animals have to keep safe from _ _ _ _ _ _ _ _ _.
4 An adult mayfly usually lives for just a few _ _ _ _ _.
5 Most species of animal have males and _ _ _ _ _ _ _.
6 All mammals care for their babies and feed them _ _ _ _.
7 Reptiles and birds lay _ _ _ _ _.

1 Complete the sentences.

> nymphs   mate   egg   exoskeleton   larvae

1 Almost all insects start their life in an _____.

2 Some baby insects look very different from their parents. These baby insects are called _____. Other baby insects look like their parents. They are called _____.

3 A young insect has a hard cover called an _____.

4 When insects are ready to produce young, they need to find a _____.

2 Write correct sentences.

1 Insects are large animals like butterflies and bees.
   <u>Insects are small animals like butterflies and bees.</u>

2 A young insect grows very slowly.
   _____

3 Most insects change by incomplete metamorphosis.
   _____

4 Female crickets and grasshoppers sing to find a mate.
   _____

5 Termite queens lay up to 3,000 eggs every day.
   _____

3 Complete the sentences.

1 There are more than a million s <u>pecies</u> of insect in the world.
2 A young insect grows inside an egg, and then it h_____.
3 Some insects grow wings that get bigger every time they m_____.
4 A pupa is like a closed c_____.
5 When insects become adults, they are ready to b_____ and produce young.
6 Male fireflies make special l_____ in their body.

4 Match the parts of sentences.

1 Many insects change in amazing ways…   c
2 Larvae and nymphs are very small…   ☐
3 When a larva is ready to change into an adult,…   ☐
4 The larva changes into an adult…   ☐
5 Many insects are careful…   ☐
6 Beetle eggs are usually yellow, green, or black so that…   ☐

a to keep their eggs safe.
b its exoskeleton comes off.
c during their life.
d they are camouflaged.
e that looks completely different.
f when they hatch.

3 Other Invertebrates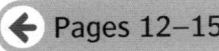

1 Match. Then write complete sentences.

some female octopuses	live	when they are twelve months old
all earthworms	eat	after their eggs hatch
young earthworms can	lay	silk to make webs
baby octopuses	use	in the open ocean
female octopuses	are	about 200,000 eggs
spiders	die	their old shell after molting
lobsters often	mate	hermaphrodites

1 <u>Some female octopuses lay about 200,000 eggs.</u>
2 _____
3 _____
4 _____
5 _____
6 _____
7 _____

2 Complete the sentences.

> oxygen   strings   months   water   eggs   predators

Many female octopuses put their eggs in _____ from the top of their dens. They keep their eggs safe from _____. They carefully push _____ over the eggs so that they get enough _____. The octopuses do not eat for up to ten _____ when they are caring for their _____.

3 Order the words. Then answer the questions.

1. and lobsters / Are / invertebrates? / spiders
   <u>Are spiders and lobsters invertebrates?</u>
   <u>Yes, they are.</u>

2. lay / Do / eggs? / earthworms
   _____
   _____

3. own / earthworms / fertilize / eggs? / Can / their
   _____
   _____

4. the ocean? / baby / at / octopuses / of / live / the bottom / Do
   _____
   _____

5. of / the top / life / Is / at / dangerous? / the ocean
   _____
   _____

4 Complete the sentences.

1. Spiders put lots of _ _ _ _ around their eggs to make a special cover, called a _ _ _ _ _ _.
2. Most spider eggs _ _ _ _ _ after a few days or weeks. The baby spiders, or _ _ _ _ _ _ _ _ _ _, grow fast.
3. The female lobster carries her eggs hidden under her _ _ _ _.

4 Fish ← Pages 16–19

1 Write the words. Then complete the sentences.

besrevetart <u>vertebrates</u>   sfni _____   koly _____

esac _____   tasodrper _____   hupoc _____

1 Fish are <u>vertebrates</u> that are cold-blooded.

2 Inside every egg there's a bag of food called the _____.

3 Female seahorses lay their eggs into a special _____ on the male's front.

4 Some sharks lay their eggs in a hard egg _____ to keep them safe.

5 Most young fish don't have _____, so they can't swim well.

6 Many _____, like seals and birds, hunt young fish.

2 Order the words.

1 live / All / water. / in / fish / and breathe
   <u>All fish live and breathe in water.</u>

2 of / fish / lay / Female / eggs. / can / hundreds
   _____

3 their / hide / try / often / eggs. / to / Fish
   _____

4 for / fish. / very / is / Life / young / dangerous
   _____

5 never / their / fish / Most / parents. / see
   _____

3 Circle the correct words.

1 Fish are **cold-blooded** / **warm-blooded** / **hot-blooded**.
2 A female tuna fish can lay up to six **hundred** / **thousand** / **million** eggs at one time.
3 Most small fish grow into adults a few **days** / **months** / **years** after hatching.
4 Fish need to find mates so that they can **eat** / **breed** / **swim**.
5 Salmon usually live in **the ocean** / **rivers** / **waterfalls**.
6 When salmon swim back to their breeding places, they change color from silver to **blue** / **yellow** / **red**.

4 Number the sentences in order (1 = first, 7 = last).

1 It lives in the ocean. ☐
2 It swims up the river, and sometimes jumps up waterfalls. ☐
3 The young sockeye salmon hatches from its egg. ☐ 1
4 When it is ready to breed, it swims back to the river where it hatched. ☐
5 It dies. ☐
6 It swims along the river to the ocean. ☐
7 It breeds. ☐

5 Amphibians  Pages 20–23

1 **Complete the sentences.**

> tadpoles   skin   metamorphosis   gills   water   midwife
> lungs   adult   eggs

1 Amphibian larvae breathe in water through special _____. Then they change into adults with _____. This change is called _____.

2 The male _____ toad carries _____ on his back until they are ready to hatch. The young frogs and toads that hatch from eggs are called _____.

3 Most _____ amphibians can breathe through their _____ and their lungs. They can only do this if it's wet, so most amphibians live near _____.

2 **Match the parts of sentences.**

1 Salamanders, toads, and frogs...
2 Usually, amphibians live in water...
3 Amphibian eggs...
4 Most amphibians...
5 At first, tadpoles...

a have a sticky cover.
b don't have legs or feet.
c for the first part of their life.
d are all amphibians.
e don't care for their eggs.

3 Complete the questions. Then write answers.

> What   How many   ~~When~~   What   Why

1 __When__ do some amphibians hibernate in colder countries?
   They hibernate in winter.

2 _____ eggs do amphibians lay?
   _____

3 _____ does the male midwife toad carry on his back?
   _____

4 _____ is life dangerous for eggs and tadpoles?
   _____

5 _____ does the male Darwin's frog keep in his throat?
   _____

4 Complete the sentences.

1 Amphibian eggs have a sticky cover, and they f_____ in water.
2 Tadpoles b_____ through gills.
3 An adult frog looks completely d_____ from a tadpole.
4 Amphibians can only breathe through their skin if it's w_____.
5 Male frogs c_____ and shout to tell the females that they are ready to b_____.

6 Reptiles ← Pages 24–27

1 Complete the words.

1 s n a k e

2 c _ _ _ _ _ _ _ _ e

3 t _ _ _ _ e

4 l _ _ _ _ d

2 Order the words. Then write *true* or *false*.

1 in / reptiles / water. / Some / live

_____   _____

2 from / reptiles / eggs. / Most / hatch

_____   _____

3 lay / a / Females / eggs / place. / in / cold, dry / their

_____   _____

4 a lot / usually / eggs. / lay / Reptiles / of

_____   _____

5 mud and / big / a / Alligators / from / make / leaves. / nest

_____   _____

6 once / old / their / snakes / lose / a year. / skin / Most

_____   _____

3 Answer the questions.

1 How do pythons keep their eggs warm?
   _____

2 How does the female Nile crocodile carry her babies to water?
   _____

3 How often do most snakes lose their old skin?
   _____

4 Why do male crocodiles blow bubbles in the water?
   _____

5 How do snakes find their mate?
   _____

6 What does the stinkpot turtle do to make predators go away?
   _____

4 Complete the sentences.

> mate   predators   tail   scales   color   parents

1 A reptile's skin is dry and covered with special _____.
2 Many eggs are eaten by _____.
3 Crocodiles and alligators are very good _____ after their eggs hatch.
4 Monitor lizards fight each other for a _____.
5 A lizard can break its _____ off to escape from a predator.
6 Some chameleons can change _____ so that predators do not see them.

7 Birds Pages 28–31

1 Match the birds with the sentences.

> songbird   blue-footed booby   ostrich
> ~~frigate bird~~   cuckoo   bower bird

1 It pushes its throat out like a balloon.   _frigate bird_
2 It shows its big feet to females.   _____
3 It sings to females.   _____
4 It builds a special place with twigs.   _____
5 It lays eggs in other birds' nests.   _____
6 Its eggs are the biggest bird eggs.   _____

2 Write sentences with these words.

1 birds / only / animals / feathers
  Birds are the only animals that have feathers.

2 male birds / many different things / find / mate
  _____

3 birds / very hard / build / nests
  _____

4 many birds / nests / high places / trees and cliffs
  _____

5 chick / ready to hatch / breaks the shell / special 'tooth' / beak
  _____

6 birds / feed / chicks / keep / safe / can / care / themselves
  _____

3 Write correct sentences.

1 There are about 900 different species of bird.

_____

2 All birds can fly.

_____

3 The male bird lays its eggs in the nest.

_____

4 If you stand on an ostrich egg, it will break.

_____

5 Birds feed their parents and keep them safe.

_____

6 Birds that migrate fly to colder places for winter.

_____

4 Complete the sentences.

1 Baby birds called c_____ come from eggs.

2 Birds are the only animals that have f_____.

3 All birds have w_____.

4 Some birds build their nests on the g_____. These birds are usually brown and speckled, so they are well c_____.

5 Birds sit on their eggs to keep them w_____.

6 Baby cuckoos p_____ other eggs or chicks out of the n_____.

8 Mammals ← Pages 32–35

1 Write the mammals.

1. $i_fe_sg_rf^a$ _giraffes_
2. $r_ad_lep_os$ _____
3. $l_op_ra\ e_bs^ar$ _____
4. $n_ah_let_sp^e$ _____
5. $o_sok^an_ga_r$ _____
6. $l_oe^pp_e$ _____
7. $s_we^rs_h$ _____
8. $s_alig^lo_r$ _____
9. $te_ra^tan_se$ _____

2 Complete the sentences. Use the words from Activity 1.

1. Male _giraffes_ fight with their head and neck to show which animal is the strongest.
2. _____ carry their babies on their back for the first year.
3. The gestation time for _____ is only two weeks.
4. Male _____ make marks on trees with their claws.
5. When baby _____ are born, they climb into their mother's pouch.
6. Baby _____ stay near their mother until they are ten years old.
7. _____ dig special dens in the snow for their babies.
8. The gestation time for African _____ is 22 months.
9. _____ hunt some animals and damage their habitats.

3 Order the words. Then answer the questions.

1 often fight / do / with / male / Why / each other? / mammals
   Why do male mammals often fight with each other?
   They often fight with each other to win a mate.

2 mammals / food / need? / do / What / baby
   _____
   _____

3 baby kangaroos / pouch? / long / their / stay / How / do / mother's / in
   _____
   _____

4 mammals / do / learn? / baby / How
   _____
   _____

4 Complete the sentences.

1 All mammals have fur or _ _ _ _ _.
2 Most baby mammals grow _ _ _ _ _ _ their mother's body. They get _ _ _ _ and oxygen from a special part of the body called the _ _ _ _ _ _ _ _.
3 Life is very _ _ _ _ _ _ _ _ _ for a lot of animals. Many are killed by _ _ _ _ _ _ _ _ _.
4 Many animals die before they become _ _ _ _ _ _, but if they _ _ _ _ up, then they can produce young.

After Reading ← Pages 3–35

1 **Check your answers to Activity 1, page 3.**

   1 = Some   2 = young   3 = in her mouth
   4 = is born   5 = a mate   6 = frog

2 **Complete the puzzle.**

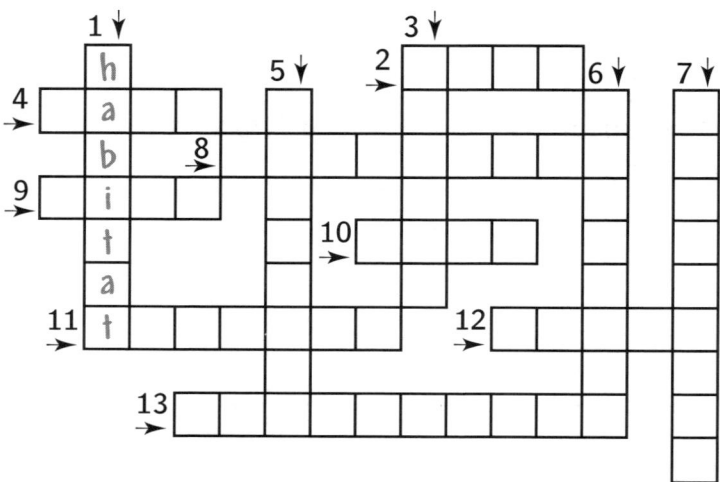

1 A ___ is the place where an animal lives.
2 Most adult amphibians can breathe through their ___.
3 A ___ is a very small animal with eight legs.
4 ___ is the opposite of dangerous.
5 All vertebrates have a ___.
6 Birds are the only animals that have ___.
7 The Nile ___ carries her babies insider her mouth.
8 A ___ is an animal that eats other animals.
9 Mammals produce ___ to feed their babies.
10 Birds can keep their chicks safe in a ___.
11 A young frog is usually called a ___.
12 Salmon swim up rivers to ___.
13 Moths and butterflies can smell ___ from 2 kilometers away.

3 Write the words. Then find and write the page.

1 These are baby insects that look very different from their parents. _____larvae_____   _page 8_

2 This is a small bag of food inside every fish egg. _____   _____

3 These snakes put their body around their eggs to keep them warm. _____   _____

4 These are animals that eat plants. _____   _____

5 This bird lays its eggs in other birds' nests. _____   _____

6 Spiders use this to make webs and cocoons. _____   _____

7 These animals fight with their head and neck to show which is the strongest. _____   _____

8 This is the hard cover around an insect. _____   _____

9 Some amphibians do this in winter when they are cold and they have no energy. _____   _____

10 These are animals that have no backbone. _____   _____

11 This reptile can change color so that predators do not see it. _____   _____

12 This is the biggest fish in the world. _____   _____

4 Complete the sentences.

> big ~~bigger~~ biggest big enough bigger too big

1 Most vertebrates are much __bigger__ than invertebrates.

2 When snakes and lizards grow, they get _____ for their skin, and the old skin comes off.

3 The two _____ groups of animals are vertebrates and invertebrates.

4 The Darwin's frog keeps his tadpoles in his throat until they are _____ to swim away.

5 Some animals, like the blue whale, are very _____.

6 Most young fish have to find food for themselves so that they can grow _____.

5 Complete the sentences. Use *can* or *have to*.

1 Sometimes salmon __have to__ jump up waterfalls.

2 Female fish _____ lay hundreds of eggs.

3 Animals _____ keep safe from predators.

4 Some chameleons _____ change color.

5 Most adult amphibians _____ breathe through their skin.

6 When reptiles are ready to breed, they _____ find a mate.

7 Whale sharks _____ weigh more than 21 metric tons.

8 Birds often _____ travel to and from their nest hundreds of times a day.

6 Complete the chart using words from **A**, **B**, and **C**.

A birds   invertebrates   ~~amphibians~~   mammals

B eggs   ~~tadpoles~~   nests   silk

C snow / babies / warm and safe
die / lay / eggs
~~wet / lakes or rivers / breed~~
push / other chicks / nest

Frog	They are __amphibians__. Young frogs are called __tadpoles__. They go to __wet places like lakes or rivers to breed__.
Spider	They are _____. They produce _____. Many spiders _____.
Cuckoo	They are _____. They lay their eggs in other birds' _____. When the baby cuckoo hatches, _____.
Polar Bear	They are _____. They do not lay _____. They dig special dens _____.

My Book Review

Title of this book: _____

Name of the author: _____

This book is about the _____ of different animals.

Questions about this book

1 What new words did you learn from this book? (Write six words.)
   _____
   _____

2 What was the most interesting animal in the book? Why?
   _____
   _____

3 Have you ever seen any of the animals in this book? Where?
   _____
   _____

What I like about this book

My favorite chapter was _____.

My favorite picture was _____.

My scores for this book (draw ☺, ☺☺, or ☺☺☺)

Interesting book ○○○   Interesting cover ○○○

Interesting pictures ○○○   Fun to read ○○○

Which book do you want to read next? _____